# Why Were All
# The Werewolves Men?

*For Lindsay on Robyn's Birthday 7th May 1998 from Granny.*

# Why Were All
# The Werewolves Men?

poems by

## Richard Stevenson

Thistledown Press Ltd.

Canadian Cataloguing in Publication Data
Stevenson, Richard, 1952 -

Why were all the werewolves men?

Poems.
ISBN 1-895449-30-8

I.  Title.

PS8587.T479W4  1994    jC811'.54   C94-920070-0
PR9199.3.S747W4   1994

Book design by A.M. Forrie
Cover and inside illustrations by Gail Mikla
Typeset by Thistledown Press Ltd.

Printed and bound in Canada by
Hignell Printing
Winnipeg, Manitoba

Thistledown Press Ltd.
633 Main Street
Saskatoon, Saskatchewan
S7H 0J8

This book has been published with the assistance of The Canada Council and
the Saskatchewan Arts Board

*These poems are for the*
*Stevensons, Booths,*
*Jordans, Polets, and Speeds —*
*their little monsters,*
*wherever they might be;*
*and for their planet,*
*its undiscovered creatures,*
*its oddities.*

# Contents

# Where Does The Ogopogo Go?

Where does the Ogopogo go
when it gets cold and snows?

Does he

swim under ice
to a cold paradise?
Bump his poor noggin
in Lake Okanagan
looking for holes
to probe with his nose?

Or does he

wiggle his toes,
put on warm clothes,
dig trenches in autumn
and sit on the bottom?

And what does

a famished lake creature eat
when there's no frozen meat
but ratsicles or duck toes,
do you suppose?

Does he

make people pies,
sit around with the guys:
old hibernating frogs,
deadheads and logs?

                        Does he
stay green and amphibious,
or get purple reptilious,
drag out his old wings,
human luggage and things
from his wiggly, watery closets
and remove the snail deposits?

                        Does he
mope in the mud,
eat duck weed and crud,
or pick up his phone,
call the Serpents in Rome?
Where does the Ogopogo go
when it gets cold and snows?

                        Does he
loaf in Lomé, Togo and
get an oh-so-vogue-o Togo tan?
Eat mangoes and bananas,
monkey meat and yams?
Or find a big castle,
avoid all the hassle,
eat that dungeon delight,
fair maidens at night?

Emerald, amphibious,
most rambunctilious —
where does the Ogopogo go
when it gets cold and snows?

# The Beast of 'Busco

In Churubusco, Indiana, certain travellers say
There lives a turtle the size of a truck
that happily dines on a diet of duck
and hapless mammals that happen his way.

All day, he hangs low, up to his nose
in noxious swamp gas and muck,
flatulent bubbles, slimey cold guck
that unctuously oozes up from his toes.

He maintains his repose 'til a duck drifts by
or he spies some floating delectable delight
or boat bottom roughage to help expedite
his digestion of children and chunks of blue sky
that taste ever so tasty in June or July.

# Cadborosaurus

Cadborosaurus — or Caddy for short —
lives in the ocean
and loves to cavort.

She frolics with coho, gobbles down cod.
Happy and healthy,
though she looks a bit odd:

Flared nostrils, cool dreadlocks, great horsey grin —
"Yo, fishes!" she says.
"Slip me some fin!"

"Ooo, I gots me a great crick in the neck —
five of 'em, in fact,
but — hey — what the heck —

Backstroke, butterfly, breaststroke, or crawl;
tumbleturn, slaptag —
babe, I do 'em all!

But should some human choogle into view —
gimme high five, waves,
I best boogaloo.

A series of humps, a dorsal, a plunge —
I's hittin' the seafloor
to hide in the grunge.

Ain't no way I's a specimen, y' dig?
Later, Charlie Tuna —
The can's not my gig.

# Loch Ness Nestor Needs Nellie Now!

The Loch Ness monster some have said
is getting old and ought to wed.

He's not some dapper dauntless kid
with hopped up hormones and active id.

Too tired to part what hair he has,
to gussy up and all that jazz,

he pops a lily pad on his pate
and leaves his lair at half-past eight.

He lets his whiskered jowls drop,
his sagging serpent coils flop.

He lolls and rolls about the shoals
and drapes the boa of his soul

over choppy trough and crest,
splashes in the jewels the sun takes west.

And some have heard him moan at night,
have seen him stretch himself upright,

and heard him wail from the pit of his belly,
"Oh where, oh where art thou, sweet Nellie?"

From top to bottom, and shore to shore,
they've watched him search since days of yore.

Without a lass, this woeful lad
has also lost his mom and dad.

He cozies up to gumboots and tires,
hub caps, tins, whatever conspires

to wink or as much as glint his way
or hint of the lass who swam away.

# Jenny Haniver

Oh Jenny Haniver,
Who could you be
That sailors made monsters
To name after thee?

Baby dragon or basilisk?
Winged serpent or devil?
Only the sailors know
Who's on the level.

Part dead ray . . .
part dead skate. . . .
Needle and thread. . . .
Bad blind date.

Oh Jenny Haniver,
Who could you be
That sailors made monsters
To name after thee?

# The Bunyip

To the Aborigines,
the bunyip's very real:
a demon, god, or spirit,
something you must feel.

To all the other Aussies,
'e's principally a figment
out of the famous dreamtime
of those of darker pigment.

"Why search for the bunyip?"
they are wont to say,
meaning a thing's impossible,
there's no truth they can assay —

As if truth were a mineral —
something you could hold,
a loadstone or a tiger skin
worth its weight in gold.

Some say it's a long-necked seal;
some believe it's a manatee
or unknown funky dugong
that got cut off from the sea.

It might just be
a hippopotamus —
wallowing in the Queensland mud
from top to bottomus,
or a particularly nasty otter,
not doin' what he oughter,
bellerin', splashin',
churnin' up the water.

All I know is that
there were creatures in my creel:
seven struggling fish, mate,
and they seemed very real!

And if you want to tell me
a nightmare creature took 'em,
or that I'm drunk or dreamin' —
and never even hooked 'em,

Fine.  O.K.  I'm goo goo
ga ga in dreamtime —
Only, tell me this, Jake:
Who drooled?  And why the slime?

# How To Catch The Giddyfish

It was my father's fondest wish
to catch the silly giddyfish,
but though he tried lures, rod and reel,
He always came home with an empty creel.

He tried purse nets and fine mesh weirs,
wetsuits and scuba tanks and spears;
skippered trawlers, seiners, punts —
but never caught a one.   Not once.

The major problem, he told me,
is the giddy's elasticity;
it can stretch through any hole,
bounce off any gaff or pole.

So then I got this perfect plan —
fish as good as in the pan:
Cut a big hole in the ice
(a seven-footer should suffice).

On the surface, float the bait;
grab an oar, then sit and wait.
When the giddy takes it, bop it one,
and it will bounce to kingdom come.

His fellow giddies, one and all
will race to catch the bouncing ball —
Ker-splish, ker-plop, right out of the hole.
You won't even need a gaff or pole.

Delicious giddyfishy meals
will jump the hoop like circus seals,
leap through the ice, onto the grill,
so everyone can get his fill!

# Alligators In The Sewer

Al the alligator
was just a little guy.
He had a toothy winsome grin
and a glinting yellow eye.
He looked so very wistful
lolling there alone —
Jenny had to have him
for her very own.

George was incubated
from such a little egg.
His shell, so frail and weak,
soon sported head and leg.
Jill pined for him all week.
What could her poor folks say?
She whined, cajoled, and begged,
eventually got her way.

Cuthbert was suave and smiled —
had perfect pointy teeth.
What trouble could he be?
Wanda's heart threw him a wreath.
Cuthbert, for his part,
was cool as a cuke and green.
He seemed to Wanda wonderful,
the best petstore pet she'd seen.

Now Al and George and Cuthbert grew
in length and girth, in grins and pounds
as twin-chinned gators often do
when fed the best ground rounds.
Now, Jen and Jill and Wanda knew
that beef would soon go up in price,
so they flushed the gators down the loo,
with a week's supply of plump pet mice.

And Al and George and Cuthbert?
What did they get for their pains?
The craziest ride on a waterslide,
and a tour of the city's drains!
The mice came tumbling afterward
like vending machine snacks,
but soon the kids ran out of change;
it was time the pets made tracks.

And trudge and crawl and slither and swim
down the sewer pipes they did,
and amid the sludge and effluent,
in the deepest darkness hid.
Sad, without any sun to grace
their lovely reptilian scales,
they began to lose their colour,
eat goldfish, rats, and snails.

Not a great diet for a gator,
but what's an albino guy to do
when he cannot buck the sewage tide
or find a solid thing to chew?
A gator needs his nutrients —
now that you can't deny —
and rats get big in sewers
and aren't in short supply.

As time went by our threesome thrived,
and though soon blind, they clawed at Braille,
met Sue and John and Erik's pets
and scribed an ending to this tale.
They courted and sparked the gator girls—
hearty babes these dames were too—
and made albino baby broods
in still, warm pools below the loo.

Now listen kids to my advice.
The lesson here may slip away
just like a languid lizard can.
A gator's eyes can often stray
from little snacks to little hams,
so when you squat on your own loo,
beware of gators down below.
They like rump roast and not tofu.

# Hapyxelor

I'm Hapyxelor, the Monster of Muskrat Lake.
I'm pleased to make your acquaintance.
Though some find me loathsome,
I'm really quite wholesome,
or was, that is, for the most part, of late.

But now I've got bulges
where once I had bilges
Plugged pores and sores
where once I had doors
portholes and floors
for my mind.

Cancerous tumors
are replacing the rumours
of this forty-foot body design.

All kinks in the hose,
toxins that repose
in these aching fat lobes
of this adipose tissue of mine,

I've got growths on my growths
lobes to my nose
knobs on my toes
sagging flesh hose
warty ear lobes
lumps in my nodes
and, you guessed 'er, Chester,
under my chest there,
under that hummock
that once was my stomach,
completely infestin'
my entire intestines
and makin' their nests in
my poor indigestion,
those slimey cold climby
wiggly cold squiggly
persistent persnickety
wickedly tickley
slithery dithery
drunken old lumpen
clumpin' and bunchin'
sippin' and suppin'
old nematodes.

I've got stumpy appendages
lumpy compendages
saggy suspendages
gross anatomy and
mind bendages
so many intendededs . . .
I don't know my head
from my toes.

And, yes, three eyes and one horn
a cry of forlorn
triangular head
to which is wed
all the flotsam and jetsam
of jettisoned medicines
e. coli and golem
of whachamightcallem
leachates and wastes
that got into my lake.

So now when I'm cruisin'
it's my trail you're confusin'
for my tail my tux and my ties.
You'll excuse my size
forgive my appearance
and give me some clearance —
a wide berth if you please —
though I can't find my knees
to bend or to crook or to scrape.

Muskrat Lake is my home
and though I'm alone
and it's getting too late
in my lifetime to mate,
I can always mutate. . . .

# Pugwis Gillman's The Name

In Thetis Lake Park
where the waters run dark
the newts and the frogs
like to sit on old logs
and the geese and the swans
honk at the fawns,
gabble and bray
at loons that get in the way.

It's peaceful and calm,
the fish scull along,
sun gracing their scales
while they admire their tails,
and dragonflies hover,
the lily pads cover
pickerel seeking the shade
while sunfish bask unafraid.

Some skinny dip here,
think there's nothing to fear:
the water's so cool
and the fish, as a rule,
are completely composed,
nip nobody's toes
or think it rude
to swim about in the nude.

The ducks are nonplussed
when their feathers get mussed,
and they bob and they preen
in flotillas serene
as the sun glints gold
from the zephyr-stroked shoals
that lap at the shadowy shore
and swallows conduct a leisurely score.

But don't be deceived
by this peaceful scene,
for beneath the last duck
buried in muck
is a most loathsome,
completely unwholesome,
terrible, pugnacious beast
that loves a mammalian feast.

Even now it is thinking
of what wine to be drinking,
what place settings it needs
for drowned-boy-and-weeds,
and how nice 'tis to floss
with green Spanish Moss,
once it's popped an eyeball or three,
and gobbled up giblets with glee.

Pugwis Gillman's his name,
though few humans can claim
the unforeseen pleasure
of dining at leisure
with his amphibious clan.
Half-frog and half man,
his handshake is fishy but firm,
his smile makes pickerel squirm.

He'd as soon eat your face
as set you a place
or partake of cocktails
or before-dinner ales.
Though often not choosey,
he's left victims woozy,
ensconced in gloomy little pubs,
b-babbling fish tales to their suds.

# IM, The Two-Headed Snake

I am I, Instinct Black Rat Snake.
I am I, Instinct Black Rat Snake.
Best leave the rat on my plate, Jake!

I am M, natty dread Mind, mon.
I am M, natty dread Mind, mon.
Feed me, rude boy, and be gone!

We're IM, two dread heads, Jim.
We're IM, two dread heads, Jim.
Tussle and Fight, Irie ites, me and him.

You feed I, I go keep M's belly full.
You feed I, I go keep M's belly full.
M's belly be full, e go push, I pull.

I & M Black Rat Snake does give and take,
Get down on im belly & moan da two-head ache.

# Huntin' Hodag

Who dat?  Who dere, scufflin', shufflin' about?
Best beware, believe it be na Prock,
o' else na hungry, hairy hodag, boys,
clawin', scrat'in' at dis bare scabby rock.

What does na Hodag eat?  How big e be?
E likem scalawag piccanin'
and does reach six feet from 'is ugly head
to na tip of 'is tail, my chillen,

and e does have na long claws and sharp teef,
na better for tear am na meat, see.
E go pluck out your eyen eat am
quick as you spy am 'n' holler b'gee.

Dem back be cover wid na great big spike,
and in na twig wood be hard to see,
but dem no have am knees; you go tag am quick,
you go get am na drop on dis bad beef.

Dis hodag bring plenty money, for true.
You catch am, shore na white man go pay
for put am in 'is zoo.  Same for na Prock
and na Guyanoosa too, dem say.

Dem white folks like na monster beef, you see.
Dem oogle and dem ogle long disting,
and dey scream, "Mo' Hodag! Bring am na Prock!"
Cus Critters go make dem jump and sing.

Who dat? Who dere? Hodag, lowdown critter,
done et my sister and bit my bro'
'fore I caught am nappin'. Das wha'appened.
Das da story, see; da whole dang show.

You go dress up dis your mutt, e pass for
na Guyanoosa o' Hodag, see.
Dey turn na light down low, folks dey pay
for see what dem no can say. Is easy.

Some time na white man no have am monster;
dey jus keep dem folk waitin' for see,
den someone yell "De Guyanoosa's loose!"
and dey gaggle like geese, scream and flee.

Dis time, we go gettim real Hodag, boys.
We go make dem holler ever' day.
We bring na house down. Dem go pay and pay,
den we git, 'fore Hodag come our way.

# Don't Touch That Rumpifusel!

It might look like a mink stole
wrapped 'round that old white pine.
You'll wonder how it got there,
want to wear its fur so fine.

Resist the temptation, please!
And don't — I entreat you —
drape it 'round your shoulders.
Necks are most uncomely blue.

Yes, yes, you heard correctly.
Rumpis are most tender creatures:
they'll wrap their rapture 'round you
and squeeze away your features.

# The Legend of Minhocao

A hundred years ago
in the state of Maranhao
the Brazilians lived in fear
of the monster Minhocao.

A gigantic worm it was —
at least fifty feet in length.
Ten feet around, they say —
and talk about amazing strength —

All sheathed in boney plates,
it bored through stony ground
like a kid poking holes in butter,
and made a terrible rumbling sound.

It re-routed great long rivers,
dug tunnels and deep trenches,
undermined whole houses,
farm buildings and strong fences;

it rampaged under forests,
uprooted many trees,
left fields of frightened cattle
sunk up to their weak knees.

The farmers grew despondent,
but what could so few men do?
Cats caterwauled and old dogs barked,
roosters raised a hullabaloo.

Rumours spread far and wide
like butter spreads on bread,
covered the countryside in gloom
as the worm exhumed the dead.

Witnesses swore on on their mothers' graves
the Minho dismembered men
and kept mutilated remains
in a subterranean den.

Farmers boiled vat upon vat of water
to flush the Minhocao free,
used flamethrowers and grenades
to help clear its dread debris.

They dynamited caverns,
tried deadly poison gases,
re-doubled all their efforts,
made many careful passes.

Alas, this came to nought.
Not a worm gave up the ghost,
though, sadly, pasture land
had been turned into burnt toast —

until one clever strapping lad
devised a brand new plan
better than any dreamt up
by science or canny man.

Why not leave the poor worm be —
go where the river flows?
Try mining for precious metals
wherever Minho goes?

Perhaps the monster's good —
Really , you must admit,
it makes a stronger drill
than any diamond bit.

Such a cheap efficient force,
I'm sure we can agree,
would cut down needless waste
and help our poor economy.

So Minhocao Mines was born,
thrived and grew apace
while tourist dollars flooded in
and blessed this troubled place.

Now the Minhocao eats the dirt
and passes diamond stools,
while people gather droppings
and filter filth like fools.

The land, I'm sad to say,
still looks like old Swiss cheese,
but the cows can make milk shakes —
on the hoof now, if you please!

# Jackalope

The jackalope of the western slope
of the back of East Snówdin
is most curious, folks,
but, I assure you, no hoax
or I'm not the King of Lódin.

True, this antlered hare,
as I am sure you're aware,
is retiring and shy,
springheeled and spry,
and, of course, exceedingly rare.

This is no reason
To assume that this season
you won't bag a few —
at least spot one or two
while you're puffin' and wheezin'.

Yes, the thinner the air,
The better you'll fare
detecting the habits
and presence of rabbits
you'd like so much to ensnare.

# The Tazelwurm

Look out, Hazel! Look out, Nirm!
Here comes the crazy tazelwurm!

Heads up, Fred! Watch out, Mabel!
It's in the soup! It's on the table!

Stand back, Jack! Get down, Betty!
It's sidling up to your spaghetti!

Hello, Harvey! Good Night, Sam!
It's in the streets; it's on the lam!

Watch out! It's poisonous: it bites!
It may be mangy or carry mites.

Whatever, it moves like a snake with legs —
or is it a lizard with vestigial pegs?

Eats bugs and slugs, lives in a cave —
is that any way for a worm to behave?

Maybe it lives inside a tube,
every day gives itself a lube.

Lord knows, and he's not telling me,
but the tazelwurm sure is a sight to see.

*Bergstutzen*, *springewurm*, *stollenwurm*
Mountain stump, jumping worm, tunnel worm:

it has so many names and tricks,
hides under rocks, in bundles of sticks;

We've often seen 'em, but never caught 'em;
Maybe if we could tell the top from bottom. . . .

Lives in the valleys of various alps —
Bavarian, Austrian, Swiss — if that helps.

Good luck finding one.  They're rare, indeed:
reclusive, shy, contrary little velocipedes.

# Whirling Whoompus

Beware the whirling whoompus, friend.
A strange and active beast is he —
you'll never see one still or penned.

They long to whirl most dervishly
and never stop or even pause
to let us get a gander, see.

So whether they have teeth or claws
or fur or feathers, no one knows,
though they obey no signs or laws,

for as the cyclone wreaks its row
of scattered dreams and broken homes
the Whoompus reaps what others sow.

Wherever the Whirling Whoompus roams
you'll see a trail of scattered bones
and measure death in megaohms.

So man the dikes, get on the phones!
Beware this typhoon devil's rage
for what a Whoompus takes it owns!

# Mokéle Mbêmbe

In the swamplands of Zaire
where the white man seldom goes
a monster named Ma BEM be
squelches mud between her toes.

Built like a brontosaurus
on a much much smaller scale,
she boasts a ten-foot neckline
and a gorgeous ten-foot tail.

Her skin, they say, is brownish-grey
and smooth as a baby's bottom.
And as for ways of catchin' rays
and attracting mates, she's got 'em!

With grace and four great hips to sway,
there ain't no sultry sauropod
in the whole Congo Chorus Line
can beat her action or her bod.

No hipper hippo can sashay
like her.  No elegunter phunt
can blow a meaner, sassy solo
than our Mokéle when she's blunt.

Chipekwe they call her. Bronto Queen.
Got the sweetest smackin' Bronto lips
that ever swilled a swamp o' grits.
Yeah! Pop yo' fingers, bump yo' hips!

Gonna get down, do the Bronto Stomp!
Tromp down some reeds! Shake some trees!
Ooo yeah! Shimmy shimmy coco bop!
Gonna part the weeds for her main squeeze!

Become methane or fossil bone?
Hold the phone! She's not compost!
Gonna swish her Mesozoic dinohips!
Ooo baby. She's heavy. She's the most!

Mokéle Mbêmbe, baby! Ooo, M'Koo —
love the way you eat yo' liana fruit!
Mbulue M'bêmbe! What I say!
You're cute. Got some science to refute!

# The Man-Eating Tree of Madagascar

The Mkodos, of Madagascar, some say
are a very unusual race —
oh my, yes, a very unusual race.

They traipse about entirely naked,
have only faint vestiges of tribal relations,
and practise no religion but pagan obeisance

to a man-eating tree they willingly feed
with great glee. Oh, yes, willingly feed —
for so they really believe, the devil tree must be appeased.

The tree, you see, has great strapping leaves —
just the sort a voracious cannibal needs
to cover its mouth while it eats.

Oh my, yes, and lest it belch with indigestion
and spew a most disagreeable half-eaten intestine
or make some other such offending suggestion,

it sups slowly and daintily with six transparent palp-
itatingly perfect stamen-like straws, and only needs help
in arranging the naughty unruly truly detestable whelp

in the acidic cup of its most assiduous petals,
and all it spits out are the bones and base metals
of cheap indigestible jewels and watches, etceterals.

An eight-foot ananas-like plant, Dr. Karl Liche explains,
with bulbous base and intoxicating nectar that makes insane
any sacrificial maiden who hallucinates for her pains

and dies an excruciating death bound in reticular coils
of subtle, sinuous, incessantly wriggling pistils and foils
while the men yell "Tsik! Tsik!" and take for their spoils

the richest red dyes blood ever gave petals and brocades
the like of any soft velvet in emerald Madagascan glades,
for the Mkodos are, indeed, a most unusual race.

# Roundel: Bigfoot Is Coming

Bigfoot is coming, and he's horribly hungry too!
He's smelly and he's hairy, and he's humming
A savage song of dumplings and peppered people
stew.
   Bigfoot is coming!

His heart, the warty toad thing, is athrumming
Fetid fundo bass notes of gloppy, sloppy goo.
Mothy-bearded, cockroach-breathed, he's slumming,

Slip-slop-slogging from the burping boggy bayou;
Eyes like cornered rats, moiling and scrumming,
Scrabbling over dirty bird nests, dripping like glue.
   Bigfoot is coming!
   Coming just for you!

# The Orang Pendek

Nothing's more of a pain in the neck
than trying to please orang pendek.
Leave us tobacco, leave us food,
or we'll get abusive; we'll get rude.

At two feet five to five feet tall,
you'd think we'd be no bother at all,
but maybe the reason we make a scene
is because we're hooked on nicotine.

Can you see a monkey eating tobacco?
No wonder it drives we gugu wack-o!
Picture us traipsing 'round the jungle —
stumbling on a Rothman's. What a bungle!

It's bad enough trying to deke out man
when you all want to bag a gugu, if you can:
Sumatrans, Javanese, Americans, Dutch —
Dodging your gun sights gets a bit much!

Since Marco Polo, you all "gotta get a gugu" —
("Sorry, fella, no shaved monkey'll do.")
Has to be the real McCoy — shock of black hair,
mane down its back, all the way to there —

A gugu, a gugu, gotta get a gugu —
a gugu to gawk at, gugu goin' goo goo,
gugu goin' ga ga — gugu, gugu, gugu —
Gotta get a gugu, put 'im in a new zoo.

Jeez!  All we wanna do is pick a few fleas
off our natty backs 'n' eat 'em, if you please!
Eat some bananas, enjoy a few mañanas —
We don't need no white suits or Havanas!

Cut us some slack!  Pack up your stogies;
go back to your hole-in-ones, eagles, and bogies.
Take up lawn bowling.  Catch a few rays.
Find something else to occupy your days.

Forget slogging through this malaria pit.
Flip on the boob tube.  Park yourself.  Sit!
Find the magic kingdom in your own livingroom,
or dress up and gibber like a blue-faced baboon.

What do we care?  Just get off our case!
We don't stumble with rifles into your space,
or swim in your biffies, so don't pee in our pools.
Leave well enough alone.  We're nobody's fools.

# Not Yeti Blues

*(to the tune of " Heartbreak Hotel")*

Now since you've climbed to find me
I've found a new place to dwell
up at the top of Chang La peak
at Backbreak Rappel.
I'm so boney,
I'm so boney,
I'm so boney
I could die.

You know, it's often cloudy,
but I found myself a cave.
Still, that ain't no 'commodation
for my mate and kids to brave,
and they're so boney,
they're so boney,
they're so boney,
they could die.

The food's so scarce and rare here
(We've got no wood for fire)
so we huddle and we cuddle
and we pray we don't expire
coz we're boney,
Yes, so boney,
oh so boney,
we could die.

You know we're now nocturnal,
got to skulk down when you sleep.
We're tall and lean and hairy,
got to get ourselves a sheep
because we're boney,
yeah so boney,
we're so boney
we could die.

We ain't a.bom.in.a.ble.
We got no need to please you.
Why don't you all just leave us,
book yourselves into a zoo
'n eat baloney,
macaroni,
get so boney
that you die.

# Orange Eyes

Well, they say he's big and hairy.
Young lovers should be wary.
Ought not ever tarry
in backwoods sublunary.

Orange eyes!  Orange eyes!
Gonna catch you by surprise.

Yeah! Ain't no sprite or fairy.
Ain't no cud-chewin' dromedary.
Don't take no luminary
to see what's culinary.

Orange eyes!  Orange eyes!
Gonna g-g-gormandize.

Now I know it's customary
to keep things light and airy,
swap spit not syllabary,
nuzzle necks and scapulary.

Orange eyes! Orange eyes!
Loves her lovely angeleyes.

Don't need no road map or dictionary
when she gets all dewy-eyed and stary
and sweet talk is fragmentary,
most un-un-necessary.

Orange eyes!  Orange eyes!
What is there to verbalize?

What's the use in lachrymary
when things get passionary?
Mammals get mammalary,
forget to be cautionary.

Orange eyes!  Orange eyes!
Don't stop to philosophize.

Ain't no sanctuary
or constabulary.
Life is temporary
when you meet this adversary.

Orange eyes!  Orange eyes!
Ain't about to empathize.

Why risk a coronary?
You know this beast is scary.
Best be discretionary
to avoid the mortuary.

Orange eyes! Orange eyes!
Gonna catch you by surprise.

# Yowza Yowie Rap

Yo! My man, homo s.,
come bend an ear.
I gots me a song, babe,
you gotta hear.

Ain't gonna diss you,
Mister bipedal man.
Doan wanna kiss you
Nor bash you wid de pan.

Ain't got no jiveass
honky tonk saw.
Ain't gonna bust me
no po' honky law.

Just wanna aks you
what you gonna do
now dat you found us
starin' back at you.

Yeah!  We's yowies.
We gots us a few owies.
We suffa,
so we tuffa,
and we really had enuffa
dem nasty usin' uppa
habitat-in-tattas blues.

Dig: it ain't no big thing
dat we's awful hairy.
Yeah, we gots us big feet,
but we ain't tryin' t'be scary.

Yous all got dem fine threads —
sweaters, socks, 'n' shoes.
We gots us hairy navels
and de buck nekked blues.

We's just tryin' to eat, boss.
Ain't gots no attitude.
Give us leaves and berries,
we doan fuss wit' you.

Jus' wanna scratch we behinds,
mebbe make us a few babies,
lollygag and hang out —
ain't gots no nos o' mebbes.

Yeah!  We's yowies.
We got us a few owies.
We suffa,
so we tuffa,
and we really had enuffa
dem nasty usin' uppa
habitat-in-tattas blues.

How can we miss you
when you won't go away?
Das what we aks owselves
Day afta day.

We's tired a bein' scruffy
'n' ever'day we hafta ruff it
coppin' scoff'n roughage —
so, baby, you can stuff it!

You doan like dem apples, Jack —
Save it for the marines!
We gots to gets us healthy
and finds us some new scenes.

We comin' outta da bush, man.
We gonna get we selves some beef.
Ow teefs groun' down enough
from eatin' da poorly pesty leaf.

Yeah! We's yowies.
We gots us a few owies.
We suffa,
so we tuffa,
and we really had enuffa
dem nasty usin' uppa
habitat-in-tattas blues.

# Zana

Pity the plight of the poor Alma, Zana,
writing in chains, deep in her pen;
fed leftovers and a daily banana. . . .

Abused daily by farmer Genaba,
who makes her a slave for other men.
Pity the plight of the poor Alma, Zana.

She might as well be in Hell or Havana.
She's no hairy Houdini, just a specimen
fed leftovers and a daily banana.

Brown skin, reddish hair — she's no Diana,
no buxom Barbie ape for hirsute Ken;
pity the plight of the poor Alma, Zana.

How can this missing link reach Nirvana,
after four pregancies by four nasty men?
Fed leftovers and a daily banana,

her only prayer is for sweetness and manna.
Weary, she cowers in her filthy fen.
Pity the plight of the poor Alma, Zana
fed leftovers and a daily banana. . . .

# Goatman's Lament

Well, some folks call me Goatman;
some folks call me Baal.
They say that I'm not human,
but my real name is Al.

Yeah, once I had a lab coat
and racks of test tubes too.
I swirled my Erlenmeyers,
centrifuged my goop from goo.

I flint-lit bunsen burners
under ring clamps and retorts,
collected gas and had a blast
filling out my lab reports.

Yeah.  I was cool; I was smart.
I had beakers; I had brains
I kept in fresh formaldehyde
and sliced and dyed with stains.

*Chorus:*

*Yeah! Don't go mess with Goatman;*
*he's bad as bad can be!*
*Gonna pop your eyes and pulverize*
*your bones for fricassee!*

Oh yes, I gathered specimens —
shot up and plugged in a few.
All served my science bravely, mind,
though some died before their cue.

Once I had some lowly beasts —
some peaceful goats and sheep.
The farmers wanted bigger yields,
so I deprived the beasts of sleep.

I had no ruddy luck, of course.
They refused to chew their cud.
I had to jack them up, you see,
to drain their iron-poor blood.

I thought that while I did so
I'd lubricate their joints,
so I gave them shots of hormones
and then I changed their points.

*(Repeat Chorus)*

Alas, one goat objected,
his mouth afroth with foam.
He rammed the spike into my thigh
and pushed the plunger home.

Well, the hormones kicked in right away,
like hundred horsepower hooves.
They messed up my ol' chromosomes
and changed my genes' hot grooves.

You see me now in lover's lane
bumper jumpin' your ol' Ford.
I cannot mix with humankind,
so I'm jealous, mad, and bored.

*(Repeat Chorus)*

It may seem dumb and immature
to get my jollies frightening folks,
but what's a guy like me to do?
Tour the borscht belt telling jokes?

Find a sprig of mistletoe
and stand beneath it looking coy?
Yeah, right.  Like I'm some Romeo
with cloven hooves they call boy toy.

Gonna flex my deltoids and my pecs
for Julie in that Chevrolet,
or sing some gallant madrigal
or play bull to my O-lay!

*(Repeat Chorus)*

Gonna flash my goatish gams
past a red cape in my hands.
How gallant!  How grand I'll be!
They'll stamp their feet up in the stands!

Face it!  That's just a fantasy.
I can't come out like this today.
There's no Panela for me to meet,
it's most sad but true to say.

I'm afraid and so I make a show
of being brave and fearsome, see.
I wish I didn't mess with you.
I wish you didn't run from me.

*(Repeat Chorus)*

# Aliens in the Freezer

Ask Doctor Gee if you don't believe me.
They're little perfect people
with little perfect teeth.
They have no known diseases
and funny three-toed feet.

Gee told Newton; Newton told me.
Saucer crashed out by Mac and Jean's,
out past Roswell, near mile seventy.
Mac and Tim, the first folks on the scene,
discovered the saucer and the strewn debris.

Summer of '47 it was — yessiree —
worst storm on record then — definitely.
Tim was first to notice the casualty ETs;
two funny little guys about four-foot-three.
Grey froggy skin they had — very slippery.

Big black eyes, no ears that Gee could see;
no noses either, just nose holes, I believe.
Slit mouths, soft, gentle high-boned cheeks;
skinny arms and legs, little kiddy knees;
big and bald high-gloss egg-shaped beans.

Mac's got a souvenir too, by golly —
a scrap of some metal you oughta see.
It's not like anything I ever machined —
won't melt or dent, though it bends easily;
Light as aluminum, but strong as steel.

Ask him and see.  Ol' Ramey's boys in green
swarmed like hornets at a boy scout jamboree.
Cordoned off the site, picked 'er good 'n' clean.
They hauled away that saucer and all the debris
on the back of a flatdeck, quick as one two three.

A cover-up was ordered: "Top Security."
Witnesses escorted off — quietly debriefed.
"Repeat after me," the air brass sang with glee,
"There's no point in news boys tryin' to talk to me:
a weather balloon broke up in actuality."

Ask Doctor Gee or Newton and you'll see.
They've got some samples of strange orthography —
weird geometric glyphs for which, honestly,
we have no Rosetta Stone, no earth hypotheses.
The cover story is nothin' but twiddlededee.

In a top secret lab in hangar seventeen
at Wright Field Air Base, I'm given to believe,
the ETs lie quiet in a deep freeze —
perfectly preserved for posterity,
doctors having done a secret autopsy.

Meanwhile, out near Roswell, New Mexico, I hear,
where stars are bright and skies are always clear,
and the only pests around are kiyoots and skeeters,
ranchers 'n' rattlers, addle-pated preachers,
the facts are still facts, memory's held dear.

Men in black suits, black glasses you'll see
pretending to prospect the ol' mountain scree
while old-time ranchers with rugged blue genes
slowly get cancer from riding their bold steeds
over radiant rangeland of glowing blue mesquite.

# Ballade of Windigo

Windigo has a heart of ice,
icicle teeth and ice-cave eyes;
his breath just reeks of rotten mice
or filthy pigs in unmucked sties,
his dead-meat head haloed with flies.
A wind, he roars through the trees,
an eagle gliding in the skies:
Windigo the bone flute, Windigo the breeze.

He metes out death in a blink, a slice
of a cleaver scattering flies,
can squish your head as in a vice
then, grinning, creep along the rise
and tumble in his fog disguise
over the raised hackles of the trees,
and curdle in bowls of blood-red eyes:
Windigo the bone flute, Windigo the breeze.

The snowy owl of the moon winks twice,
fluffs his feathers to twice his size;
watches the bleating clouds of paradise
flounce and gambol across the skies.
Old as sunset, he's seen blood freeze,
knows the songs of Windigo's lies:
Windigo the bone flute, Windigo the breeze.

*Envoi*

Owl sees Windigo as a rumpled shirt,
shakes him, hangs him neat as you please;
clean as pants minus the dirt:
Windigo the wind bag, shooting the breeze.

Aliens?

Space men?

"The Good People?"

Fairies from other worlds?

Creatures from our own planet?

Who are these other beings anyway?

Kidnappers? Abductors? What do they want exactly?

Why the clinical tests?  The secrecy?

Are we just breeding stock?

Big bugs in their jars?

Where are they from?

Are they friends

or foes?

What?

# Mannegishi

*(to the tune of "Do Wah Diddy")*

There it was just a slippin' down the street,
singin' MAN NE GISHI SWISHY DOWN SQUISHY GOO,
poppin' out eyeballs and a-slurpin' its treat,
singin' MAN NE GISHI SWISHY DOWN SQUISHY GOO.

He sucked blood — sucked blood,
slurped slime — slurped slime,
and I nearly lost my mind.

Before I knew it we were fallin' in muh-uh-uh-ud;
I gave it all the things I was blee-ee-eeding from.
Now we're together nearly every single way,
Singin' MAN NE GISHI SWISHY DOWN SQUISHY GOO.

We're so yucky and that's how we're gonna stay,
Singin' MAN NE GISHI SWISHY DOWN SQUISHY GOO.

'Cause I'm fizz — I'm fizz
and he's slime — he's slime;
deadly gells are gonna rime,
singin' MAN NE GISHI SWISHY DOWN SQUISHY GOO.

Before I knew it he was schleppin' next to me,
singin' MAN NE GISHI SWISHY DOWN SQUISHY GOO.
It topped my head just as natural as could be,
singin' MAN NE GISHI SWISHY DOWN SQUISHY GOO.

We schlepped on — schlepped on
to my floor — my floor,
the we schlepped a little more.

My my my, I knew we was waddlin' in bloo-oo-oo-d,
singin' MAN NE GISHI SWISHY DOWN SQUISHY GOO.

*(repeat ad nauseam)*

# Why Were All The Werewolves Men?

Why were all the werewolves men,
with manners like my Uncle Ken:
stupid, burly mesomorphs
who preyed on women, nerds, and dwarfs?

It's bad enough they ate meat raw
and left gory leftovers people saw.
With table manners so obscene,
you'd think they'd rather not be seen.

But no.  They'd skulk their neighbourhoods
and leave blood trails throughout the woods,
announce their presence to the moon,
expect all women to faint and swoon,

to get all quivery and loose as liver
and fall into their arms and shiver
for the honour of offering up their flesh
to some hairy goof whose gears don't mesh.

Heck, if I were a woman and my date
broke out in fur at my front gate,
I'd take a spike heel to his head
or mace the jerk.  I'd  yell, "Drop dead!"

Or if night fell and a full moon
found him writhing in my room,
I'd loosen his collar at the sink,
slip him a Mickey Finn to drink.

I'd take a chisel to his pointy teeth,
haul him off to some bog or heath,
let him come to without a stitch,
fangless, hairless, in a ditch.

Let him swoon and shriek in fear
when he looks into a mirror.
Out-vamped by the feminine wiles
of a hairless were-woman who smiles

and knows how to bare her Pepsodent pearls
better than any of his goofy girls.
Someone who isn't the least impressed
by bad-breathed dweebs with hairy chests.

# Vlad Tepes

There once was a young prince named Vlad
with an instinct to torture so bad
No amount of blood
Could lessen the flood
Of the fiendish grim fancies from Dad.

Now Vlad's Dad was known as Dracul
(Roumanian for Devil or Ghoul)
And he thought it nice
To drink blood on ice
And be cruel in order to rule.

Soon Vlad Basarab (Junior's Dad)
Passed on the mad mantle of bad
And Vlad Jr. would excel
In unleashing all hell
From his flash Transylvanian pad.

Now Dracula (son of Dracul)
Had blood that ran hot and ran cool.
To prove better badness
He perfected pa's madness
And opened a new torture school.

To increase his most exquisite pleasure
He offered the peasants some leisure,
Bid each man bring a bowl
to catch the blood toll,
and make sausages townsfolk would treasure.

Now business was better than good.
The peasants made stakes out of wood,
and Vlad would impale 'em,
the sad victims regale 'im
as only their tortured souls could.

A few hundred a week he'd dispatch.
The devil himself was no match.
Kill a thou' in one go —
a most hideous show.
Every soul who'd escape he would catch.

Vlad Dracul, the impaling old ram,
he outvamped the best Hollywood ham,
overdrew his accounts
by such bloody amounts
his own bank wouldn't spot him a dram.

# Zombie Blues

Well, I woke up this mornin' with an awful achin' head.
Yeah, I woke up this mornin' with a poundin' hurtin' head.
Doc said, "You got no pulse, boy; how come you ain't dead?"

Well, I told him, "Doctor, I was feelin' pretty low."
Yeah, I said , "Doctor, I was feelin' sad and low.
Got down in my coffin; gots no place else to go."

Well, the voodoo priest he gave me a nasty wicked brew.
Yeah, the voodoo priest he gave me a nasty smellin' brew.
Paralyzed my body, said, "Son, I got a treat for you."

He dumped a snake into my crate — a tarantula too.
Mmm Hmm — into my coffin with that woolly spider too.
Said, "Need another playmate? Hope this scorpion will do."

Well, I couldn't move a muscle, but I was wide awake.
Yeah, I couldn't move a muscle, or I would surely shake.
The priest he closed the lid, said, "Dig, I ain't no fake."

Yeah, he said, "I got dis reputation I gots to uphold.
Das right boy, I got dis cash'n'carry I gots to have'n'hold.
Cants have folks complainin' my potions are too old."

"You see, boy, conditions bad; your wages gone too high.
Yeah, Mmm Hmm, life is bad; your wages hit the sky.
Gonna make you a slave, boy; you won't be askin' why."

"Yeah, you'll be my worker; have no reason to complain.
Dats right, a perfect worker; wid no vex or hex or pain.
I'll have your soul, babe, your body and your brain."

Yeah, Mmm Hmm, dats what he said before he buried me.
Yeah, I'll have your only soul, and then he buried me.
And creepy crawlers crept and crawled in ticklish villainy.

Now, I had me this ol' air tube, so's I could get some air.
Yeah, I had me this old air tube, but wasn't goin' anywhere.
All I could do, babe, was sweat, and stink, and stare.

And now my soul is in a jar and my butt is here.
Yeah, now my soul is captured and my butt is here.
Got 4 rows of dis cane chopped; got 6 more yet to clear.

I got no pulse or will or wits, but I gots me this here job.
I got no wife or kids or frien', but I gots me this ol' job.
Gonna do the zombie shuffle; gonna chop and dance and bob,

Yeah, gonna get down do the hand jive in Cap-Haitian town.
Gonna get down, do the Piltdown in this funky town.
And when I get down in the ground, ain't no one gonna frown.

Cos I'm a zero zombie, Zeke; ain't no uppa crusty snob.
Yeah, das all: a zombie, Zeke; ain't no Jim or Bill or Bob.
Gonna rot'n'stink'n'lose some parts, but gonna keep my job.
Gonna rot'n'lose some parts, gonna keep this stinkin'job.

# List of Illustrations

# The Author's Notes On Monsters

The *Random House College Dictionary* defines a monster as: 1. a fabled animal combining human and animal features, as a centaur, griffon, or sphinx.

2. any creature so ugly as to appal or frighten people.

3. any animal or human grotesquely deviating from the normal.

4. anything unnatural or monstrous.

5. Biol. an animal or plant of abnormal form or structure, as from marked malformation, the absence of certain parts or organs, etc.

6. a person who excites horror, as by wickedness or cruelty.

7. any mammal or thing of huge size.

Readers may not be aware of the precise nature of the fearsome creatures I have assembled in this book, so here are a few notes to acquaint the wary reader with them.

## Water Monsters

The OGOPOGO — or Naitaka as he was called by the First Nations people of the Okanagan region — is Canada's most well-known lake monster. The descriptions vary from a vertically undulating serpentine creature with horsey head and giraffe-like horns to a plesiosaur-like creature with broad back, long tail, four flippers, and a long neck. He is described as remarkably similar to Nessie, the Loch Ness monster of Scotland.

Add a mane, big eyes, and a curious look, move the creature to the oceans of the Pacific Northwest, and you have the CADBOROSAURUS, though some cryptozoologists suspect the reason for variance in sighting reports of sea monsters is that we've got at least eight unknown species frolicking in the seas and many legends and names describing each.

Since the early days of ocean voyages, sea serpents and sea creatures have been reported and all sorts of oddball creatures have been faked. One famous fake is the JENNY HANIVER, a skate carved up and twisted around so that its bottom-feeding mouth apparatus looks like the fearsome face of a baby-winged serpent.

Other fresh-water monsters aren't serpents or plesiosaur-like creatures at all. THE BEAST OF 'BUSCO — a supposedly existent giant turtle — has become the mascot of the folks of Churubusco, Indiana, while, in New York, the urban legend of albino alligators — supposedly the offspring of baby alligators flushed down the toilets — continue to inspire many tall tales and be recycled in literature, like Thomas Pynchon's *V*.

A Creature of the Black Lagoon — half-man, half-fish — has been reportedly sighted in little old Thetis Lake in Victoria, B.C., (I invented a name for him: PUGWIS GILLMAN) and may be a descendant of the urban mythic Frogman sighted elsewhere in the United States.

From the deep swamps of the Lake Tele region of Zaire come tales of a creature presumed to be a living dinosaur, MOKÉLE MBÊMBE, subject of the recent film, *Baby: Secret of The Lost Legend*. It is supposed to be a miniature brontosaurus with a single horn or tooth.

Also supposedly bearing a single horn or tooth is the otherwise serpentine creature, HAPYXELOR of Muskrat Lake, Canada. I imagine mine to be a mutant from all the pollution in many of Canada's bigger lakes.

Tales of lake monsters like the Ogopogo or LOCH NESS MONSTER are legion. In Canada, we have Champ, the monster of Lake Champlain; Igopogo, the monster of Lake Simcoe; Manipogo, from Lake Manitoba; Ta-Zum-ta, from Lake Shuswap; Tsinquaw of Cowichan Lake; the Lake Utopia Monster; and the Monster of Lake Pohenegamook. In the United States, tales of longish serpents and ogopogo-like creatures are no less prevalent.

The BUNYIP of Australia, if it exists, is presumed to be an undiscovered marsupial or perhaps a long-necked seal of grandiose proportions, but people assume it's an unknown amphibian or aquatic reptile. Your guess is as good as mine as to what it looks like!

# Monsters of the Woods: The Hairy Homonids

If the large lakes and seashores of the world can claim to boast a large population of unknown creatures, the woods can claim all manner of plausible and wildly implausible beasts as well.

Sasquatch sightings abound in virtually all the provinces and states that can boast a forest, huge swamp, or bottomland. In western Canada, a large hairy anthropoid supposedly occupying the eco-logical niche between the ape and our Cro-Magnon ancestors has been reported often. One theory holds that Gigantopithecus, a massive 8 – 12 foot anthropoid and our sasquatch are one in the same. Many believe there may be several subsets of the Gigantopi-thecan line or that some Neanderthalers, thought to have lived alongside their more developed bretheren, Cro-Magnon man, may not have died out. The hairy homonid descriptions are remarkably similar the world over and include monsters like Bigfoot, from the Pacific Northwest and legendary beasts from various Native tra-ditions such as D'Sonquoa (B.C.) and WINDIGO or Wendigo (Ontario). The latter are cannibal women or men who can assume misty proportions or shift their shapes to become wolves or coyotes.

Interestingly, Sasquatch sightings frequently occur simultaneously with U.F.O. activity, and so, not surprisingly, an element of the supernatural and other-worldly often gets grafted onto the BIGFOOT sighting lore. ORANGE EYES is supposed to be a nasty hairy homonid that frequents lovers lanes and picks on folks in parked cars. Goatman, a variant of the Greek god Pan, is said to do the same but be a half-goat, half-man, satyr-like creature, and there are all sorts of variants in urban mythology about how he got that way. My fanciful solution to that particular mystery is my own.

The YETI or Abominable Snowman is an aggressive cousin of the Sasquatch with the same tall, hairy appearance and retiring ways and is said to occupy the high mountains of Tibet and Nepal. I've made mine lean and hungry as a result of being pushed to higher peaks by man's steady encroachment.

In China, the Yeti's more diminutive equivalent is the Alma. My creature ZANA is said to be a half-breed Alma/man.

Particularly nasty is the Monogrande of the Venezuelan Amazon, said to tear out cattle's tongues and tear people to pieces. More placid is the Australian YOWIE, a smelly vegetarian.

Smaller intelligent ape-like creatures rumoured to live in Sumatra and Java include the ORANG PENDEK or Gugu.

## Creatures from Outer Space/ Other Dimensions

The Cree have a legend about a diminutive creature with a big head, long toes and fingers, and big saucer-like eyes. They call him MANNEGISHI and claim his purpose on earth is to trick man. Mine has decidedly bad table manners and isn't quite so playful. The Mannegishi may well be the same saucer telemetrist as Dover, Massachusetts' Dover Demon, which, in turn, bears a striking similarity to the creatures of alien abduction lore dubbed the greys (often referred to as little green men, though their skin is seldom green).

The ALIENS IN THE FREEZER are greys: little four-foot guys with wrap-around mantis-like eyes, big bald heads and skinny limbs.

A concomitant theory is the notion that the Celtic fairies and elves and European little people and leprechauns are our greys: we see what the fabric of our reality shapes as real to us, just as our ancient ancestors saw what "fit" into their consensus reality.

## Phantoms and Shape-Shifters

Phantom creatures frequently turn up where they are not supposed to exist: cougars or panthers in Surrey, U.K., kangaroos in the continental U.S., giant penguins in Florida (even a penguin might want a sun-filled holiday in the tropics), devil footprints on both sides of a wall, or disembodied Hairy Hands on the Dartmoor Strip in England.

Sometimes it isn't at all clear whether the beast we are talking about is a spirit shape-shifter or a real crypto-beast as yet undiscovered by modern science. Some mystery creatures include MNGWA, a monster cat or bear from Zaire, and the Nandi Bear or Chemosit of Kenya, a similar creature who eats only fresh brains! In other cases, a mythology has grown up around rural legends connected with real persons or odd mental states in which humans behave badly and seem to develop an unnatural craving for human blood.

Vampire mythology has its roots in the very real and very hideous impaling activities of VLAD TEPES, a fifteenth-century Roumanian monarch, and a rare disease which causes victims' gums to recede from their teeth and makes them appear pale and anaemic. Victims of this disease shun sunlight and need red blood cells, so in a true scientific sense, they are vampires. Vlad and these poor diseased recluses weren't the only psychotics or night-dwellers to suffer from blood lust though.

Nor were all the real vampires men. The Polish Countess, Elizabeth de Bathory believed that bathing in the blood of young virgins would preserve her own youthful appearance and estimates of the number of her victims in the seventeenth-century range from 300 to 650.

The WEREWOLF probably rivals the vampire as premier shape-shifter and may owe its existence to earlier tales of the European Wodewose or Wild Man, probably a primitive Neanderthaler or Sasquatch-like homonid that kept to the woods away from civilization and may have eventually migrated over the frozen landmass that once linked Siberia to Alaska.

## Fearsome Critters and Other Tall-Tale Beasties

Many of the monsters in this book have their genesis in the overactive imaginations of backwoods folk, lumberjacks, fishermen and good old boys wont to pull the wool over the eyes of generations of greenhorns in rural Arkansas, the Adirondacks, Newfoundland and anywhere else the blarney reigns supreme and oral story-telling remains a living art. Sometimes the tall tales have been supported by famous fake creations ( as in the case of the Beazel or fur-bearing trout, stuffed and mounted in many a bar ) and other times the fakes are difficult to separate from actual cryptozoological sightings because of a degree of overlap in plausibility or owing to the artistry and sheer audacity of the would-be barkers and tourist-mongerers involved (as in the case of the Minnesota Iceman, a frozen Hollywood Homonid and The Silver Lake Monster, a faked Ogopogo). More often than not, though, the creatures are wonderfully preposterous creations.

The RUMPEFUSEL, as described in my poem, is a live mink stole-like creature of sorts that specializes in strangling those who innocently wrap it round their necks. The HODAG is a fearsome mammal of the Wisconsin swamps, with sharp teeth, long claws, spiked back and tail — and has often been faked by suiting up a dog in the requisite armour and turning the lights down. My poem recreates one such scam in an invented backwoods dialect perhaps related to Mississippi Black English.

The JACKALOPE is an antlered hare — the subject of many a faked photo, and a very photogenic creature. The WHIRLING WHOOMPUS is a creature that spins in a dervish cyclone that moves so fast you can't see it or make out its features. GIDDYFISH are rubbery fish that follow each other like bouncing balls and are notoriously difficult to catch because of their elastic ways. THE MAN-EATING TREE OF MADAGASCAR is probably a hyperbolic extension of a known carnivorous plant, a totally fictitious creation that comes down to us from African expedition lore. I've tried to

98

employ a suitable Kiplingesque diction and mock-racist tone to give it the flavour it deserves.

## Unknown Vertebrates

There are many vertebrates that don't walk upright on two feet and unless we got down on our hands and knees in all the hard-to-reach ecological niches of all the uninhabited or unfrequented jungles, mountains, and byways of the world, we wouldn't be likely to spot them. The assumption that all the world's flora and fauna have now been discovered, tagged, and catalogued is patently absurd when you consider that more than a tenth of the world's land mass has yet to receive a human footprint.

The TAZELWURM is a snake-like legless or nearly legless lizard that is wont to coil up under rocks in the high Alpine regions of mountainous Europe. Or is it? Some say it's a worm; some say it's a snake. I say, "Who cares? Let it recoil from our mad lot as long as it can!"

# Acknowledgments

Some of the poems in this collection have previously appeared in the anthologies *The Canadian Anthology of Modern Verse For Children* (Edited by I.B. Iskov), *Canadian Children's Annual, Number 11* (Potlatch Publications Ltd., 1985); *Jumbo Gumbo: Songs, Poems and Stories For Children*, Edited by Wenda McArthur & Geoffrey Ursell (*Coteau Books*, 1989); *Senary* (Fallen Octopress, 1992); and in the small magazines and Sci-Fi/ speculative literature newsletters *Artwalk Magazine, Chameleon, The Crosstime Journal, Distant Horizons, Lost Magazine, Power Animal, Scifant* (Luna Ventures), and *Whetstone*.

My thanks to the editors for their encouragement and support.